"Tony's message comes straight from the heart: By doing simple acts of kindness for others, we can't help but lift ourselves up, too."
—Ted Danson,
actor and President, American Oceans Campaign

"God bless Tony Robbins for having the heart to share himself with others."
—Christauria Welland Akong,
Migrant Outreach, San Diego, California

"This book is more than a note from a friend; it's an indispensable guide to taking charge of your life."
—Arnold Schwarzenegger

Notes from a Friend

A Quick and Simple Guide to Taking Charge of Your Life

Anthony Robbins

A FIRESIDE BOOK
Published by Simon & Schuster
New York London Toronto Sydney Tokyo Singapore

F

FIRESIDE
Rockefeller Center
1230 Avenue of the Americas
New York, NY 10020

First Fireside Edition 1995

Edited by Just Write
Cover photo by Bill Bernstein

Reprinted by permission of the
Anthony Robbins Foundation:
9191 Town Centre Drive
Suite 600
San Diego, California 92122
(619) 535-9900, ext. 244

FIRESIDE and colophon are registered
trademarks of Simon & Schuster Inc.

Manufactured in the United States of America

3   5   7   9   10   8   6   4   2

Library of Congress Cataloging-in-Publication Data
Robbins, Anthony.
Notes from a friend :
a quick and simple guide to taking charge of your life /
Anthony Robbins. — 1st Fireside ed.
p.   cm.
1. Success—Psychological aspects.   I. Title.
BF637.S8R556   1995
158′.1—dc20   95-19436
CIP
ISBN 0-684-80056-X

To those who understand that life's greatest gift is

love, and life's greatest joy is sharing it

Especially for the volunteers and staff of the

Anthony Robbins Foundation, whose efforts

consistently improve, change, and save lives

ABOUT THIS BOOK

Notes from a Friend, based on the concepts and stories in Anthony Robbins' bestsellers *Awaken the Giant Within* and *Unlimited Power*, was originally published by the nonprofit Anthony Robbins Foundation in 1991. Designed to assist those who are going through "tough times," it simplifies the material in these larger books and offers readers understanding and support in the form of a few simple steps for immediately improving the quality of their lives.

In conjunction with the foundation's annual Basket Brigade, this book is distributed free of charge to needy families and individuals. The event, which takes place in Canada and the United States, is a volunteer effort to deliver food, clothing, and other resources to those in need during the Thanksgiving holiday. If you would like to participate in this cross-continental effort, please call 619-535-9900, extension 244.

All author's royalties from this new edition are being donated to the Anthony Robbins Foundation to support the Basket Brigade and other volunteer events. You can read more about the foundation on pages 101–103 in this book.

THANK YOU!

Thank you for your investment in this book. Because of your interest in improving your own life, you have already contributed to improving other people's lives. Your contribution supports the Anthony Robbins Foundation's volunteer efforts every year to provide food, education, and other resources for more than 150,000 people in need throughout the United States and Canada.

I wrote this book years ago in a very simple, down-home style as a part of our foundation's annual Thanksgiving Basket Brigade. As you'll read in the next few pages, this holiday means a lot to me: it's not only a national tradition, but a personal one for me, too. It's a time when, more than ever, a sense of gratitude for the blessings in my life overflows into a desire to reach out to others. So this book is exactly what it's called: a note from a friend, to be read at any time of the year by anyone who just needs or wants a bit of inspiration from someone who cares. It offers some encouragement to those who need a reminder of life's basic truths and the stimulation of a few good ideas about how to deal with whatever challenges face them.

Ironically, the simplicity of this little book has always appealed as much to the thousands of volunteers who hand it out as to the recipients. Many have wanted this book for themselves as a reminder of the fundamentals it takes to truly succeed in creating and enjoying a quality life. What's more, a bit of informal research has shown me that many people never read my more comprehensive works, *Unlimited Power* and *Awaken the Giant Within*, because they're intimidated by the size of the books (more than 400 pages each).

As a result, I've decided to update and republish *Notes from a Friend* for the general public. If you're already a student of my work, there may be little new here. Yet there seems to be a special effect on those who read it: they gain a new perspective as they review the material in this easy-to-read, accessible style. If you're new to my work, I hope you'll find that this is a fun introduction, and I encourage you to look into the resources from which *Notes from a Friend* is drawn.

We tend to forget that all of us come up against tough times, times when we feel as though events and circumstances have more control over our lives than we do. Sometimes we just *feel* down and out. Being dismissed from a job, for example—even if we still have our homes and loved ones—can cause us a great sense of loss. The challenges of our own lives can seem so immense that we also tend to forget the frustrations of people around us.

We are not alone. Part of a quality life, part of true success, is learning to appreciate and consider the emotional struggle of our neighbors. This gives us a greater sense of gratitude for our own lives, even for our own struggles. Ultimately, the only way to experience the richness of life is to live in an attitude of gratitude: to appreciate what you have and what you can give. The best way to ensure your happiness is to assist others in experiencing their own.

Since you're reading this book, you have already given something significant. As an "honorary member" of our Basket Brigade, you are sharing in our efforts to give more than food. *Notes from a Friend* gives people food for thought, a simple way of looking at their lives, and an avenue for beginning to change and improve them.

Thank you for helping. I hope not only that this book assists you in immeasurably improving the quality of your life, but that it may inspire you to help others as well.

CONTENTS

What would happen if, in the next few pages, you could learn some simple steps that would allow you to feel happier, earn a better living, or improve virtually any area of your life?

Introduction
ONE MAN'S STORY

On Thanksgiving many years ago, a young family awoke with a sense of foreboding. Instead of looking forward to a day filled with gratitude, they were preoccupied by thoughts of what they did not have. At best, they would scrape together a meager meal on this day of "feasting." If they had contacted a local charity group, they would have had a turkey with all the trimmings, but they hadn't. Why? Because they, like many other families, were proud people. Somehow they would make do with what they had.

The difficult situation led to frustration and hopelessness, then to irreparable, harsh words between the mother and father. The eldest son felt devastated and helpless as he watched the people he loved most become more and more angry and depressed.

Then destiny intervened . . . a loud and unexpected knock at the door! The boy opened it and was greeted by a tall man in rumpled clothing. He was grinning broadly, carrying a huge basket brimming with every conceivable Thanksgiving delight: a turkey, stuffing, pies, sweet potatoes, canned goods—everything for a holiday feast!

The family was stunned. The man at the door said, "This is from someone who knows you're in need and wants you to know that you're loved and cared for." At first, the father of the family didn't want to take the basket, but the man said, "Look, I'm just a delivery person." Smiling, he set the basket in the boy's arms, turned to leave, then called over his shoulder, "Have a great Thanksgiving!"

In that moment, this young man's life was forever changed. With this simple act of kindness, he learned that hope is eternal, that people—even "strangers"—really do care. The sense of gratitude he felt moved him deeply, and he swore to himself that someday he'd do well enough to give something back to others in a similar way. And by the time he was eighteen years old, he had begun to fulfill that promise. With his scant earnings, he set out to purchase groceries, not for himself, but for two families he had learned were in dire need of food. He then drove to deliver them, dressed in an old pair of jeans and a T-shirt, intending to present the gift as if he were a delivery boy. When he arrived at the first dilapidated house, he was greeted by a Latina woman who looked at him suspiciously. She had six children, and her husband had abandoned the family only a few days before. They had no food.

The young man offered, "I have a delivery for you, ma'am."

He then went out to his car and began to carry in bags and boxes overflowing with food: a turkey, stuffing, pies, sweet potatoes, canned goods. The woman's jaw dropped. The children, when they saw the food being brought into the house, let out shrieks of delight.

The young mother, who spoke only broken English, grabbed the young man by the arm and started to kiss him all over, saying, "You gift from God! You gift from God!"

"No, no," the young man said. "I'm just the delivery boy. This is a gift from a friend." Then he handed her a note that said,

This is a note from a friend. Please have a wonderful Thanksgiving—you and your family deserve it. Know that you are loved. And someday, if you have the chance, please do well enough to do this for someone else and pass on the gift.

The young man continued to bring in bag after bag of groceries. The excitement, joy, and love reached a fever pitch. By the time he left, the sense of connection and contribution moved the young man to tears. As he drove away, looking back at the smiling faces of the family he'd had the privilege to help, he realized that his story had come full circle, that the "horrible day" from his youth was actually a gift from God, guiding him, pointing him toward fulfillment through a life committed to contribution. With this one act he began a quest that continues to this day: to return the gift that was given to him and his family and to remind people that there is always a way to turn things around, that they are loved, and that—with simple steps, a little understanding, and massive action—whatever challenges exist now can be turned into valuable lessons and opportunities for personal growth and long-term happiness.

How do I know so much about this young man and his family, not only about what they did, but also how they felt? Because he is me.

I wrote this book because I want you to know that someone cares about you. I want you to know that no matter how daunting or overwhelming your circumstances may seem, you truly can turn things around. You can turn the dreams you once had into reality. How? By tapping into a power that's inside of you right now as you read these words. This power within you can change anything in your life literally in a matter of moments. **All you must do is unleash it.**

How can I say this to you with such conviction?

All you must do is unleash this power.

Simply because I've used this same power to change my own life on a massive scale. A little more than a decade ago, I was struggling and completely frustrated, with little or no hope. I was living in a cramped 400-square-foot bachelor apartment in Venice, California. I was lonely, miserable, and 38 pounds overweight. I had no plans for my future. I felt that life had dealt me a miserable hand and that there was nothing I could do to change it. I was financially broke and emotionally bankrupt. I felt overwhelmed, helpless, and defeated.

I'm here to tell you, though, that in less than one year, I changed it all. I lost 30 pounds in less than 30 days. And I kept it off, because I didn't just go on a diet, I changed my mindset. I trained my body into peak physical condition. I developed the confidence that was necessary to make it through the tough times and really achieve the goals I'd dreamed about. My secret was focusing on the needs of other people. I constantly asked the question "How can I add something of value to people's lives?" Through this thought process, I became a leader. I realized early on that I couldn't help others change if I couldn't change myself. Not only was the secret to living giving, but to give, I had to become a better person. In the process of becoming more, I attracted the woman of my dreams, married her, and became a father. I went from living hand-to-mouth to more than a million-dollar net worth in less than one year. I moved from my run-down apartment to my present home: a 10,000-square-foot castle overlooking the Pacific Ocean.

But I didn't stop there. As soon as I'd proved I could help myself, I immediately sought out the most profound ways to help others. I began to search for role models, those who could create change with lightning-like speed. These peak performers were some of the top teachers and therapists in the world, those who helped people with their problems in one or two sessions instead of one, two, or more years. Like a sponge, I learned as much as I could and began applying what they taught me immediately. I began to develop a series of strategies and understandings of my own.

Since then, these techniques have led me to work with more than a million people from forty-two nations in the world, offering them the "tools" and coaching to help them turn their lives around. This incredible privilege and opportunity to share my work has extended to a wonderful diversity of people, from blue-collar workers to blue bloods from royal families around the globe, from presidents of countries to presidents of companies and presidents of the PTA, from movie stars to professional athletes and sports teams, from moms and medical doctors to children and the homeless. And through my books, tapes, seminars, and television shows, I've reached literally tens of millions of people. In every case, my goal has been to help people take control of and immediately increase their quality of life.

I don't tell you this to impress you but to impress upon you how fast things can change. Once we understand what shapes our thoughts, feelings, and behavior, all it takes is consistent, intelligent, massive action. With this book, I'm volunteering to be your coach in making any of the changes you desire.

Positive Thinking Is Not Enough

We all have dreams, don't we? We all want to believe that we're special, that somehow in our lives we can make a difference, that we can touch our family, our friends, or other people in some special way. At one time in our lives, we all had an idea of what we really wanted and what we really deserved.

Too many people, though, forget their dreams when they face life's challenges. They set their aspirations aside, forget that they have the power to shape their future, then lose their confidence and hope. It's been my life's goal to remind people—people just like you and me —that the power to change anything lies sleeping within us. **We can wake up this power and bring our dreams back to life, *starting today*.** This book will give you some simple tools that can truly assist you in making this happen.

Of course, positive thinking is a great start. Certainly you want to focus on how to turn things around—on *solutions*—rather than on how things are so "wrong." **But positive thinking alone is not enough to turn your life around.** You must have some strategies, some step-by-step plans for changing how you think, how you feel, and what you do *every single day you're alive.*

Isn't it true that all of us want to change or improve something in our lives? Almost all the changes we want to make fall into one of two categories: either we want to change the way we *feel* about things (we want to have more confidence, we want to overcome our fears, we want to rid ourselves of frustrations, we want to feel happy, or feel better about things that have happened in the past), or we want to change our *actions* (we want to do something different, such as to quit smoking, drinking or procrastinating). The big problem is that although everyone wants to make these changes, *very few people know how to produce a change—and make it last.*

With this book, I'd like to help you get started in the direction of making positive change on a consistent basis. I'm not promising you the world out of this one little book. But I *am* promising you that you can, absolutely, take control and begin to change the quality of your life using some simple steps that you'll learn in the following pages. You'll also be able to apply these simple steps in helping your family members and friends.

The only thing that's necessary to make this work for you right now is to begin to believe that it *is* possible to change. The past doesn't matter. Whatever hasn't worked in the past has nothing to do with what you'll do today. What you do *right now* is what will shape your destiny. Right now, you must be a friend to yourself. You can't "beat yourself up" about what's happened; instead, you must immediately focus on solutions instead of problems.

Are you willing to begin the journey? Then let's get started. Let's begin to change our lives by understanding what to do when we are . . .

Lesson One
FEELING OVERWHELMED . . .
HOW TO TURN IT AROUND

Often in life, events occur that we truly can't control. The company we're working for "downsizes" and we get laid off. Our spouse leaves us. A family member becomes ill, or someone close to us dies. The government cuts a program we've depended on. In these situations, we may feel as if there is simply nothing we can do to make things better.

Maybe you've had the experience of trying everything you knew to get a job, to help your family, to find your soulmate, or just to feel happier. But nothing seemed to work. When we try a new approach, try our best, yet we still fail to reach our goal, often we fear trying again. Why? Because we all want to avoid pain! And nobody wants to fail again. Nobody wants to give his or her all, only to be disappointed. Often, after many of these experiences of disappointment, we stop trying! We get to the point where we believe that *nothing* will work.

If you find yourself at the point where you're not even willing to try, you've put yourself in a place called "learned helplessness." You've literally learned—or taught yourself—that you're "helpless."

The good news is that you're wrong. You *can* make things happen! You can change anything in your life today by changing your perceptions and changing your actions.

"I am not discouraged, because every wrong attempt discarded is another step forward."
—Thomas Edison

The first step to turning your life around is getting rid of this negative belief that you can't do anything or that you're helpless. How can you do that? Often the reason that people say they can't do something is that they've tried things in the past that haven't worked. But remember—and I've used this phrase again and again throughout my life—**YOUR PAST DOES NOT EQUAL YOUR FUTURE.** What matters is not yesterday but what you do *right now*. So many people are trying to drive into the future using a rearview mirror to guide themselves! If you do that, you'll crash. Instead you must focus on what you can do *today* to make things better.

Persistence Pays

Many people tell me, "I've tried *millions* of ways to succeed, and nothing works!" Or, "I've tried *thousands* of ways!" Think about it. They probably haven't even tried hundreds of ways to change things, or even dozens. Most people have tried eight, nine, ten ways to make a change, and when it hasn't worked out, they've given up.

The key to success is to decide what's most important to you and then take massive action each day to make it better, even when it doesn't look as if it's working.

I'll give you an example. Have you ever heard of a guy named Colonel Sanders? Of course you have. How did Colonel Sanders become such an unbelievable success? Was it because he was born wealthy? Was his family rich? Did they send him to a top university like Harvard? Maybe he was successful because he started his business when he was really young. Are any of these true?

The answer is no. Colonel Sanders didn't begin to fulfill his dream until he was 65 years old! What drove him to finally take action? He was broke and alone. He got his first Social Security check for $105, and he got mad. But instead of blaming society or just writing Congress a nasty note, he started asking himself, **"What could I do that would be valuable for other people? What could I give back?"** He started thinking about what he had that was valuable to others.

His first answer was, "Well, I have this chicken recipe everyone seems to love! What if I sold my chicken recipe to restaurants? Could I make money doing that?" Then he immediately thought, "That's ridiculous. Selling my recipe won't even pay the rent." And he got a new idea: "What if I not only sold them my recipe but also showed them how to cook the chicken properly? What if the chicken was so good that it increased their business? If more people came to see them and they made more chicken sales, maybe they would give me a percentage of those additional sales."

Many people have great ideas. But Colonel Sanders was different. He was a man who didn't just think of great things to do. *He put them into action.* He went and started knocking on doors, telling each restaurant owner his story: "I've got a great chicken recipe, and I think if you use it, it'll increase your sales. And I'd like to get a percentage of that increase."

Well, many people laughed in his face. They said, "Look, old man, get out of here. What are you wearing that stupid white suit for?" Did Colonel Sanders give up? Absolutely not. He had the #1 key to success; I call it *personal power.* **Personal power means being persistent in taking action: Every time you do something,**

**you learn from it, and you find a way to do it better
next time.** Colonel Sanders certainly used his personal
power! Instead of feeling bad about the last restaurant
that had rejected his idea, he immediately started focusing on how to tell his story more effectively and get better
results from the next restaurant.

How many times do you think Colonel Sanders
heard no before getting the answer he wanted? **He was
refused 1,009 times before he heard his first yes.** He
spent *two years* driving across America in his old, beat-
up car, sleeping in the back seat in his rumpled white
suit, getting up each day eager to share his idea with
someone new. Often, the only food he had was a quick
bite of the samples he was preparing for prospective
buyers. How many people do you think would have gone
for 1,009 noes—two years of noes!—and kept on going?
Very few. That's why there's only one Colonel Sanders. I
think most people wouldn't get past twenty noes, much
less a hundred or a thousand! Yet this is sometimes what
it takes to succeed.

If you look at any of the most successful people in
history, you will find this common thread: They would
not be denied. They would not accept no. They would
not allow anything to stop them from making their vision,
their goal, a reality. Did you know that Walt Disney was
turned down 302 times before he got financing for his
dream of creating "The Happiest Place on Earth"? All the
banks thought he was crazy. He wasn't crazy; he was
a visionary and, more important, he was committed to
making that vision a reality. Today, millions of people
have shared in "the joy of Disney," a world like no other,
a world launched by the decision of one man.

When I lived in my crummy little apartment, washing my dishes in the bathtub, I had to keep reminding myself of these kinds of stories. I had to keep reminding myself that **NO PROBLEM IS PERMANENT. NO PROBLEM AFFECTS MY ENTIRE LIFE. THIS TOO SHALL PASS IF I CONTINUE TO TAKE MASSIVE, POSITIVE, CONSTRUCTIVE ACTION.** I kept thinking, "Even though my life looks terrible right now, there are many things to be thankful for, like the two friends I have, or the fact that I have all my senses, or that I can breathe fresh air." I constantly reminded myself to focus on what I wanted, to focus on *solutions* instead of problems. And I remembered that no problem affects my entire life, even though it may look like it right now.

So I decided I would no longer believe that my whole life was screwed up simply because I had financial difficulties or emotional frustrations. I decided that there was nothing wrong with me, but that I was simply in "lag time." In other words, I knew that if I were to continue nurturing the seeds I had planted—continue doing the right things—I would make it out of this winter of my life and into spring, when I would reap the rewards of years of seemingly fruitless efforts. I also decided that doing exactly the same things over and over again and expecting a different result was insane. I had to try something new, and I had to keep on until I found the answers I needed.

My message to you is simple, and in your heart you know it's true: **Massive, consistent action with pure persistence and a sense of flexibility in pursuing your goals will ultimately give you what you want, but you must abandon any sense that there is no solution.** You must focus immediately on the actions you can take today, even if they are small ones.

This makes sense, doesn't it? So why don't more people follow the advice of the Nike ad and just do it? The answer is that they've been shut down by fear of failure. But I've discovered something wonderful about failure. . . .

Lesson Two
THERE ARE NO FAILURES

Right now it's time for you to make a *decision.* Right now you have to promise yourself that you'll never indulge in feelings of being defeated or depressed again. This doesn't mean that you have to be unrealistic about the challenges before you. It simply means that you now understand that the emotions of defeat and depression stop you from taking the very actions that can change your life. You must believe that even though things may look impossible now, you can turn them around. **You see, we all have problems, disappointments, and frustrations, but it's** *how we deal with our setbacks* **that will shape our lives more than anything else we do.**

I'd like to share with you a wonderful example of this principle in action. Many years ago, a young man wanted to be a famous musician, so he quit school and went out on the road. Getting a job was a pretty tough gig for a high school dropout with no experience. He found himself playing piano and singing in some of the seediest bars around town, giving his heart and soul to people who were so drunk they didn't even notice he was in the room. Can you imagine the frustration and humiliation he must have felt? He was depressed and emotionally destroyed. He had no money, so he slept in laundromats. The only thing that kept him going was the love of his girlfriend, a woman he knew was the most beautiful on earth.

But one day she left him, too—and he felt that his life was over. He decided to commit suicide. But before

he committed the act, he tried to get some help by check-
ing himself into a mental hospital. In that hospital, his life
changed—not because he was "cured," but because it
scared him to see just how bad things could be! He realized that he had no *real* problems. And that day, he prom-
ised himself that he would never, ever allow himself to
get that down again. He would work as hard as he had to,
for as long as he had to, to finally become the successful
musician he knew he could be. **No person, no disappointment was worth committing suicide over. Life
is always worth living. There's always something to
be grateful for.**

So he kept at it. The rewards did not come at first,
but eventually they did. In fact, today his music is known
around the world. His name is Billy Joel.

You and I need to constantly remember that **GOD'S
DELAYS ARE NOT GOD'S DENIALS,** that there are
no failures, that if you try something and it doesn't work,
but you learn something from it that can help you be
more effective in the future, then you've truly succeeded.

In fact, there's a saying that's helped me through the
years:

**SUCCESS IS THE RESULT OF GOOD
JUDGMENT.**

**GOOD JUDGMENT IS THE RESULT OF
EXPERIENCE.**

**EXPERIENCE IS OFTEN THE RESULT
OF BAD JUDGMENT.**

Keep at it! If we keep striving to make things better,
and we learn from our "mistakes," then we will succeed.
Now let's look at what causes us to take action. . . .

Lesson Three
THE UNSTOPPABLE YOU: DECISION MAKER

I've said throughout this little book that there is a power to change any part of your life. So where is it? How do we engage it? We all know that to get new results we have to take new actions, but we must realize that all our actions are fathered by a decision: **the power of decision is the power of change.** Again, it's true that we can't always control the events of our lives, but we can control what we decide to think, believe, feel, and do about those events. We must remember that every moment we're alive, whether we admit it to ourselves or not, a new set of choices, a new set of actions, and a new set of results are merely a decision or two away. Most of us forget that we have this power to choose. **ULTIMATELY, IT'S OUR DECISIONS, NOT THE CONDITIONS OF OUR LIVES, THAT DETERMINE OUR DESTINY.** How you live today is the result of who you've decided to spend time with, what you've decided to learn or not to learn, what you've decided to believe, your decisions to give up or your decisions to persist, your decisions to get married or have children, your decisions about what to eat, your decisions to smoke or drink, your decisions about who you are and what you're capable of—all of these have literally controlled and directed your life. If we sincerely want to change our lives, then we've got to make some new decisions about what we stand for and what we're going to do ... and what we're *committed* to.

When I use the word *decision,* I mean a real and

conscious choice. Most people say, "Well, I decided that I'm going to lose some weight," but that's too general, not specific enough. They're just stating a preference; in other words, they're saying, "I'd *like* to be thinner." A real decision is made when you cut off any possibility except what you've committed to do, when you will not look back, when you will not even consider the alternative of giving up.

Let me give you a great example of a man who understood the power of a real decision, someone who, once he decided, would not give up. His name is Soichiro Honda: founder of the Honda Corporation, the maker of Honda cars and motorcycles. Mr. Honda never allowed tragedy, problems, challenges, or the twists and turns of circumstance to get in his way. **In fact, he often decided to see some of the biggest obstacles in his way as mere hurdles in the race to reach his goals.**

In 1938, Mr. Honda was a poor student who had a dream of designing a piston ring that he would sell to and manufacture for Toyota Corporation. Every day he

Mr. Honda often decided to see some of the biggest obstacles in his way as mere hurdles in the race to reach his goals.

would go to school, and all night long he would work on his design, up to his elbows in grease. He spent what little money he had on his project, and it still wasn't finished. Finally, he hocked his wife's jewelry to continue.

After years of effort he finally designed the piston ring he was sure Toyota would buy. When he took it to them, they rejected it. He was sent back to school to suffer the humiliation of his teachers' and friends' telling him what an idiot he was for designing such a ridiculous gadget.

Was he frustrated? You bet. Was he broke? Yes. Did he give up? *No way.*

Instead, he spent the next two years continuing to find ways to make the piston ring better. He had the key formula to success:

1. He decided what he wanted.

2. He took action.

3. He noticed whether it was working or not, and when things weren't working out,

4. He kept changing his approach. He was *flexible* in the way he went about things.

Finally, after two more years, he refined his design, and Toyota actually bought it!

In order to build his piston factory, Mr. Honda needed concrete, but the Japanese government was gearing up for World War II, so none was available. Once again, it looked as if his dream would die. It seemed no one would help him. Again, did he quit? Absolutely not. He had decided to build this factory. Since giving up was not an option, he got together a group of his friends, and for weeks they worked around the clock trying different approaches until they found a new way to manufacture concrete. He built his factory and was finally able to produce his piston rings.

"But Wait, There's More. . . ."

The story doesn't end here. During the war, the United States bombed his factory, destroying most of it. Instead of feeling defeated, he rallied all his employees. He said, "Quickly! Run outside and watch those planes. What they'll do is drop their fuel cans out of the sky. We need to find out where they drop them and get those cans, because they contain the raw materials we need for our manufacturing process!" These were materials they couldn't get anywhere in Japan. **Mr. Honda found a way to use whatever life gave him.** Finally, an earthquake leveled his factory, and he was forced to sell his piston operation to Toyota. But God never closes a door without opening another one, so we need to stay alert to see whatever new opportunities life presents us. . . .

When the war ended, Japan was in total turmoil. Resources were scarce in all parts of the country—gasoline was rationed and, in some cases, nearly impossible to find—and Mr. Honda couldn't even get enough gas to drive his car to the market to buy food for his family. But instead of feeling defeated or helpless, he made a new decision. He decided he would not settle for this quality of life. He asked himself a very powerful question: "How else can I feed my family? How can I use things I already have to find a way to get there?" He noticed a little motor he had, one that was the size and type to drive a traditional lawn mower, and he got the idea of hooking it up to his bicycle. In that moment, the first motorized bike was created. He drove it to and from the market, and pretty soon his friends were asking him to make some for them, too. Shortly thereafter, he'd made so many "motorbikes" that he ran out of motors, so he decided to build a new factory to manufacture his own. But he had no money, and Japan was torn apart. How would he do it?

"It is in your moments of decision that your destiny is shaped."
—Anthony Robbins

Instead of giving up and saying, "There's no way," he came up with a brilliant idea. He *decided* to write a letter to every single bicycle-shop owner in Japan, telling them that he thought he had the solution for getting Japan moving again, that his motorbike would be cheap and would help people get where they needed to go. Then he asked them to invest.

Of the 18,000 bicycle-shop owners who received a letter, 3,000 gave Mr. Honda money, and he manufactured his first shipment. And then he was a success, right? Wrong! The motorbike was too big and bulky, and very few Japanese bought it. So once again, he noticed what wasn't working, and instead of giving up, he changed his approach again. He *decided* to strip his motorbike down and make it much lighter and smaller. He called it The Cub, and it became an "overnight success," winning Honda the Emperor's Award. Everyone looked at him and thought how "lucky" he was to have come up with this idea.

Was he lucky? Maybe, if L.U.C.K. means *L*abor *U*nder *C*orrect *K*nowledge. Today, Mr. Honda's company is one of the most successful in the world. Honda Corporation now employs over 100,000 people and outsells all but Toyota cars in the U.S.—all because *Mr. Honda never gave up.* **He never let problems or circumstances get in his way. He** *decided* **that there is** *always* **a way to succeed if you're really committed!**

Decisions, Decisions!

You and I both know that there are people who were born with advantages: they were born to wealthy parents in privileged environments; they seemed blessed with strong, healthy bodies; they were taken care of in every way you can imagine and never lacked for anything. Yet you and I also know that many of these same people end up fat, frustrated, and chemically addicted.

By the same token, we constantly meet, read about, and hear of people who against all odds have exploded beyond the limitations of their conditions by making *new decisions* about what to do with their lives. **They've become examples of the unlimited power of the human spirit.**

How did these amazing individuals do it? They all, at some moment, decided that they'd had enough. They decided they would no longer tolerate anything but the best. They made a real decision to change their lives.

What do I mean by a "real decision"? So many people say things like, "Well, I really should lose some

When you make a real decision, you draw a line,
and it's not in the sand but in cement.

weight. I should make more money. I should do something to get a better job. I should stop drinking." But you can "should" all over yourself, and things still won't change!

The only way to change your life is to make a real decision. A real decision means you cut off *any other possibility* than the one you've decided to make a reality.

If making decisions is so simple and powerful, why don't more people make them more often? Because they don't know what a real decision is. They think decisions are like a wish list: "I'd like to quit smoking," or "I wish I'd stop drinking." Most of us haven't made a decision in so long we've forgotten what it feels like!

When you make a real decision, you draw a line, and it's not in the sand but in cement. You know exactly what you want. This kind of clarity gives you the power to do even more to get the results you've decided to go for.

The people who overcome the odds and turn their lives around make three powerful kinds of decisions every day:

1. what to focus on
2. what things mean
3. what to do

Another of my favorite examples is the story of Ed Roberts. He's an "ordinary" man confined to a wheelchair who became extraordinary by his decision to act beyond his apparent limitations. Paralyzed from the neck down since he was fourteen years old, each day he uses a breathing device that he's mastered against great odds to lead as normal a life as possible, and he spends every night in an iron lung. Almost dying several times, he certainly could have decided to focus on his own pain, but instead chose to make a difference for others.

Just what has he managed to do? For the last fifteen years, his decision to fight against a world he often found condescending has resulted in many improvements in the quality of life for people who are disabled. Ed Roberts educated the public and initiated everything from wheelchair access ramps and special parking spaces to grab bars. He became the first quadriplegic to graduate from the University of California, Berkeley, and he eventually held the position of director of the California State Department of Rehabilitation, again pioneering this position for people who are disabled.

Clearly, this man chose to focus on something different from what most people in his position would focus on. **He focused on how he could make a difference.** His physical difficulties meant "challenge" to him. What he decided to do was anything that could make the quality of life for others in his position more comfortable. He absolutely committed himself to shaping the environment in a way that would improve the quality of life for all physically challenged people.

Ed Roberts is powerful evidence that it's not where you start out but the *decisions* you make about where you're determined to end up that matter. All his actions were founded in a single, powerful, committed moment of decision. What could you do with your life if you really *decided* to?

So Decide Now!

All human progress begins with a new decision. So what are some things you've been putting off, some things you know you need to do to make your life better?

Maybe it's a decision to replace smoking or drinking with jogging or reading. Or to start each day earlier and with a better attitude. Maybe it's a decision to no longer blame anyone else, and instead to figure out some new action you could take each day to make your life better. Maybe it's a decision to get a new job by finding a way to be more valuable than almost anyone else. Maybe it's a decision to study and develop some new skills that allow you to earn more or give more to your family and friends.

Right now, make two decisions you're willing to follow through on—whatever it takes. First, make one simple decision: a promise to yourself or others that you can easily keep. By making this decision and acting upon it, you'll prove to yourself that you can make even bigger decisions. You'll begin to develop strong "decision-making muscles"!

Now, make a second decision that you know will take even more commitment from yourself. Make one that inspires you. Write the two decisions in the space below, tell your family and friends the decisions you've made, and enjoy the pride of sticking to them!

Two Important Decisions I've Made
and Commit to Keeping!

1. _____

_____

_____

2. _____

_____

_____

Whether you make your decisions real or not will depend upon your ability to . . .

Lesson Four

BUILD YOUR BELIEFS AND . . . BLAST OFF!

There is a force that controls all your decisions. It influences how you think and feel every moment you're alive. It determines what you will do and what you will not do. It determines how you feel about anything that occurs in your life. That force is your *beliefs*.

When you believe something, you give your brain an unquestioned command to respond in a certain way. For example, have you ever been asked something like "Would you please get the salt?" and you walked into the kitchen thinking, "I don't know where the salt is"? You looked all around in the cupboards and finally said, "I can't find the salt." Sure enough, the person who asked you to get the salt walked into the room, stood next to you, pointed right in front of your face, and said, "What is this?" It was the salt! Was it always there? You bet. How come you didn't see it? Because you didn't *believe* the salt was there.

As soon as we have a belief, it begins to control what we can see and what we can feel. In fact, did you know that beliefs can even change the color of a person's eyes? They can. According to Dr. Bernie Siegel, the author of *Love, Medicine, and Miracles* and other books about the mind-body connection, scientists have found some interesting things about people who have multiple personalities: when some of these individuals believe that they have changed into another person, their brain is given a command that literally changes their biochemistry—and the color of their eyes changes as they switch personalities!

Beliefs can even affect your heartbeat. People who faithfully believe in voodoo will die if someone puts a "hex" on them—not because of the hex but because they give their own heart an unquestioned command to stop beating.

Do you think your beliefs can affect your life and the lives of those around you? You bet! Beliefs are very powerful, so you've got to be careful about what you choose to believe, especially about yourself. I can tell you that throughout the years, there are certain beliefs that have really helped me. Some of those beliefs I've already mentioned in this book:

- "There's always a way to turn things around if I'm committed."
- "There are no failures in life. As long as I learn anything from something, then I've succeeded."
- "God's delays are not God's denials."
- "The past does not equal the future."
- "In any moment, I can change my entire life by making a new decision."

These beliefs have directed the way I think and the way I behave. They have helped me turn things around against tremendous obstacles to create lifelong success.

"Faith is to believe what you do not yet see; the reward for this faith is to see what you believe."

—St. Augustine

What is a belief, anyway? Often we talk about things without having a clear idea of what they really are. Most people treat a belief as if it's a real thing, when it's actually nothing but a **feeling of certainty** about what something means. If you say you believe that you're intelligent, all you're really saying is, "I *feel certain* that I'm intelligent." That sense of certainty allows you to tap resources that help you act intelligently to produce the results you want. We all have the answers for virtually anything—or at least we have access to the answers we need through others. But often our lack of belief—our lack of certainty—causes us to be unable to use the capacity that resides within us.

A simple way of understanding a belief is to think about its basic building block: an idea. There are a lot of ideas you may think about but not really believe. For example, let's look at the idea that you're loving. Stop for a second and say to yourself, "I'm loving."

Now, whether "I'm loving" is an idea or a belief will come down to the amount of certainty you feel about this phrase as you say it. If you think, "Well, I'm not really loving," what you're really saying is, "I don't *feel very certain* that I'm loving."

How do we turn an idea into a belief? Let me offer you a simple metaphor to describe the process. If you can think of an *idea* as a table with only one or two legs, you'll have a pretty good picture of why an idea doesn't feel as solid as a belief. Without its legs, that table won't even stand up by itself. A *belief,* on the other hand, is a table with enough solid legs. If you really believe, "I'm loving," how do you *know* you are? Isn't it true that you have some references to support the idea? In other words, don't you have some *experiences* to back it up? Those are the "legs" that make your table solid—that make your belief *certain.*

What are some of the reference experiences you've

had that make you feel certain you are loving? Maybe someone has told you that you are a very loving person. Or maybe you do things every day that make someone else feel more comfortable, more happy, or more hopeful. Maybe you feel good toward other people, and just *feeling* loving means that you are full of love for others. But you know what? All of these experiences mean nothing until you use them to support the idea that you're loving. As you do so, the legs make you feel solid (certain) about the idea and cause you to begin believing it. Your idea feels solid, and now it's a belief.

What are some of the reference experiences you've had that make you sure that you are loving?

Once you understand how beliefs are like tables, you can begin to see how they are formed and get a hint of how you can change them, as well. First, though, it's important to note that we can develop beliefs about *anything* if we just find enough legs to support them.

Isn't it true that you have enough experiences or

know enough other people who have gone through tough times that if you really wanted to, you could easily develop the belief that people are rotten and, given half a chance, would take advantage of you? Maybe you don't want to believe this, and I'm sure you know that this kind of belief won't really get you anywhere, but don't you have experiences that could support this idea and make you feel certain about it if you wanted to?

Isn't it also true, however, that you have experiences—references—to back up the idea that people are basically good and that if you really care about them and treat them well, they will want to help you, too?

The most important question is: **Which one of these is true? It's whichever belief you decide to assemble—it's your choice.** The key, then, is to decide which beliefs will empower you and which ones will disempower you.

Beliefs are a huge source of power. *You* **can choose what to believe about yourself, and these beliefs will determine the actions you take.** The important thing is to choose beliefs that support you and give you hope and energy.

What are three beliefs that you need right now? Do you need to believe you have the confidence to handle a job interview? the strength to get out of a bad relationship? the caring to get into a great relationship? Write down at least one belief that you must adopt immediately:

I Must Believe:

_____

_____

Sometimes people say to me, "Yeah, Tony, I believed in something once—but it didn't work." How do they know for sure it didn't work? Maybe they should have given it more time.

Maybe they'd learn from this thousand-year-old story from India. It's about a farmer who has only one horse to pull his plow, and the horse runs away. His neighbors say, "That's terrible!"

The farmer says, "Maybe."

The next day, he comes back with two horses. His neighbors say, "That's wonderful!"

"Maybe," the farmer says.

His son tries to break the horses and ends up breaking his own leg. "Oh, that's horrible!" the neighbors say.

"Maybe," he says.

The next day, the army shows up to take all the men to war, but they can't take his injured son. Now the neighbors say, "Oh, you're so lucky!"

What do you think his response is? Right: "Maybe."

And the story goes on and on, as does life. If you believe in something, and it hasn't worked yet, maybe you're judging too soon. When you think you're in trouble, maybe you're not. Maybe it's only temporary.

Just remember that your ability to make these judgments wisely will depend largely on the possibilities that you envision because ...

Lesson Five
WHAT YOU SEE IS WHAT YOU GET

So many people want to change how they feel, but they don't know how. The fastest way to change how you feel about anything is to **change what you're focusing on.** If you want to feel lousy right now, it would be pretty easy, wouldn't it? All you'd have to do is think about something painful that's happened in your life and focus all your attention on it—if you thought about it long enough you'd feel lousy again.

How ridiculous! Would you sit through a lousy movie over and over again? Of course not! So why go to a lousy movie *in your mind?* This experiment just shows how easy it is for anybody to slip into lousy feelings—and how crucial it is to control your focus. Even if things are tough, you've got to focus on what you *can* do, on what you *can* control.

If you wanted to feel good right now, you could do that just as easily, couldn't you? You could focus on something that's made you happy, something that's made you feel good about yourself or your family or friends. You could focus on something that you're grateful for today. Or you could focus so intensely on the future you're dreaming of that you get excited about it in advance! That will give you the energy to start making things happen.

Let me give you a simple example. Let's say you go to a party, and you have a video camera. All night, you focus that camera lens on the left corner of the room where a couple is arguing. As you focus on it, you, too, might get caught up in their anger and unhappiness.

Since you're focusing on their rage, you're probably thinking, "What a miserable couple. What a *miserable* party."

What if, that same night at the party, you'd focused your attention on the right corner? In the right corner, there are a bunch of people laughing and joking and, instead of fighting, they're having a blast! Then if somebody asked you, "What was the party like?," you'd say, "Oh! It was a *wonderful* party!" The point is simple: There are unlimited things people can notice, but too many of us focus on what's terrible, on the things we can't control.

Steer Your Focus in the Right Direction

Can you see why focus is so important? It controls how you see the world and what you do about it. Do you think it might also control how you feel? You bet it does.

Your focus can literally save your life. One of the things that I enjoy most is racing cars. I'll never forget the most important lesson I learned in race car driving school. The teacher said, "The most important thing for you to remember is how to come out of a skid." (That's a good metaphor for life, isn't it? Sometimes we get in a skid where we feel like we're out of control.) "The key to this is very simple," he instructed. "What most people do when they start to go into a skid is focus on what they fear—the wall. Instead, you must focus on *where you want to go.*" I'm sure you've heard about people who are driving down some back road in their sports car, and all of a sudden they lose control. For miles around, there's only one telephone pole, but somehow they manage to hit it. The reason is that as soon as people lose control, they zero in on exactly what they want to avoid—and they connect with it. **The reality is that whatever you focus on you move toward.**

My instructor told me, "We're going to get into a 'skid car.' I've got a computer here, and when I push this button, your wheel will lift off the ground, causing you to skid out of control. When we skid, *don't look at the wall.* **Focus on where you want to go."**

"No problem," I said, "I understand."

My first time out on the road I was screaming along, and my instructor pushed the button. All of a sudden I started to skid out of control. Where do you think my eyes went? You bet! Right at the wall! In the final seconds, I was terrified because I knew I was going to hit it. But then my instructor grabbed my head and twisted it to the left, forcing me to look in the direction I needed to go. We kept skidding, and I knew we were going to crash, but I was forced to look only in the direction he pointed me in. Sure enough, as I focused in that direction, I couldn't help but turn the wheel accordingly. It caught at the last moment, and we pulled out. You can imagine my relief!

One thing that's useful to know about all this: when you change your focus, often you don't *immediately* change direction. Isn't that true in life as well? Often there's a lag time between when you redirect your focus and when your experience catches up. That's all the more reason to start focusing on what you want quickly and not wait any longer to solve the problem.

But back to our story. Did I learn my lesson? Not quite. The next time I headed for the wall, the instructor had to remind me loudly to look at my goal. On the third time, though, I turned my head myself. I trusted that it would work, and it did. Now when I go into a skid, *wham!* my head goes where I want it to go, the wheel turns, and

Focus on where you want to go.

my car follows. Does this guarantee I'll always succeed by controlling my focus? No. Does it increase my chances? You bet!

How does this relate to you? You and I must make sure that when problems come up we focus on solutions, that we focus on where we want to go instead of on what frightens us. **Whatever you think about most you'll experience.**

Changing focus, making decisions, and changing beliefs—does all this stuff happen overnight? Of course not. Again, it's like building up muscles. Your muscles don't just bulge out suddenly like Popeye's! It all happens bit by bit. But I guarantee you, if you change your focus even a little, your reality is going to change a lot.

Now, let's learn one of the most powerful tools for changing your focus, something I've used every day of my life since I decided to make my dreams a reality. . . .

Lesson Six
QUESTIONS ARE THE ANSWER

The best way to control your focus is through the power of questions. Do you know that asking the right question can actually save your life?

It saved Stanislavsky Lech's life. The Nazis stormed into his home one night and herded him and his family to a death camp in Krakow. His family was murdered before his eyes.

Weak, grieving, and starving, he worked from sunrise to sundown alongside the other prisoners of the concentration camp. How could anyone survive such horrors? Somehow he continued. One day, he looked at the nightmare around him and decided that if he stayed there even one more day, he would die. He decided that he had to escape. And most important, he believed that even though no one before him had escaped, somehow there was a way.

His focus changed from how to survive to asking instead, "How can we escape this horrible place?" He received the same answer over and over. "Don't be a fool! There is no escape. Asking such questions will only torture your soul." But he wouldn't accept this answer. He kept asking himself, "How can I do it? There must be a way. How can I get out of here?"

One day, his answer came. Lech smelled rotting flesh just a few feet from where he worked: men, women, and children who had been gassed and whose naked corpses had been piled into the back of a truck. Instead of focusing on the question "How could God allow something so evil to happen?," he asked himself, "How can I use this to escape?"

As the sun set and the work party left for the barracks, he pulled off his clothes and dove naked into the pile of bodies while no one was looking.

Pretending to be dead, he waited with the sickening smell of death all around him, the weight of all the corpses pressing upon him. Finally, he heard the truck engine start. After a short ride, the mountain of bodies was dumped into an open grave. He waited until he was certain no one was nearby, and then ran—naked—the 25 miles to freedom.

What made the difference between the fate of Stanislavsky Lech and that of many of the millions who died in concentration camps? Clearly there were several factors, but one difference is that he asked a different question. And he asked it over and over, with expectation, certain he would receive an answer.

That's a Good Question!

We ask ourselves questions all day long. Our questions control our focus, how we think, and how we feel.

Asking the right questions was one of the major ways I turned my life around. I stopped asking, "Why is life so unfair?" and "Why don't my plans ever work out?" **Instead, I started to ask questions that could give me useful answers.**

"Ask and you will receive. Seek and you will find; knock, and it will be opened to you."
                                        —Matthew 7:7

First, I made up some questions to solve problems. These questions prepare me to look for and find solutions whenever a problem comes up.

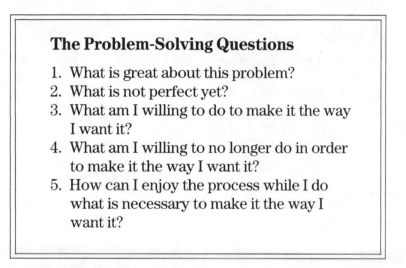

The Problem-Solving Questions

1. What is great about this problem?
2. What is not perfect yet?
3. What am I willing to do to make it the way I want it?
4. What am I willing to no longer do in order to make it the way I want it?
5. How can I enjoy the process while I do what is necessary to make it the way I want it?

If you have trouble answering any of these questions, use the word *could.* Example: "What *could* I be most happy about in my life right now?"

I also ask myself a specific set of questions in the morning when I get up and another set of questions at night before I go to sleep. They set me up for feeling great all day and end my days on a high note.

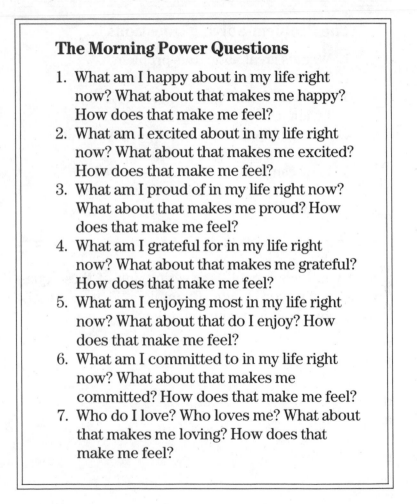

The Morning Power Questions

1. What am I happy about in my life right now? What about that makes me happy? How does that make me feel?
2. What am I excited about in my life right now? What about that makes me excited? How does that make me feel?
3. What am I proud of in my life right now? What about that makes me proud? How does that make me feel?
4. What am I grateful for in my life right now? What about that makes me grateful? How does that make me feel?
5. What am I enjoying most in my life right now? What about that do I enjoy? How does that make me feel?
6. What am I committed to in my life right now? What about that makes me committed? How does that make me feel?
7. Who do I love? Who loves me? What about that makes me loving? How does that make me feel?

The Evening Power Questions

1. What have I given today? In what ways have I been a giver today?
2. What did I learn today?
3. How has today added to the quality of my life? How can I use today as an investment in my future?

These questions have been lifesavers for me. They will help you change your focus—and can help you change your life.

The Gift of Great Questions

Once you know how to ask empowering questions, you can help not only yourself but others as well. Once, in New York City, I met a friend and business associate of mine for lunch. He was a prominent lawyer, and I admired him for his success in business and for the practice he'd built since he was a young man. But on that day, he had suffered what he thought was a devastating blow —his partner had left the firm, leaving him with tremendous overhead and not many ideas about how to turn it around.

Remember that his focus was determining the meaning. In any situation, you can focus on what will make you feel better or on what will make you feel worse —and **whatever you look for you'll find.** The problem was that he was asking all the wrong questions: "How could my partner abandon me this way? Doesn't he care? Doesn't he realize that this is destroying my life? Doesn't

These questions have been lifesavers for me.

he realize that I can't do this without him? How will I explain to my clients that I can't stay in business any longer?" All these questions already assumed that his life had been destroyed.

There were many ways in which I could have helped my friend, but I decided that I would just ask a few questions. So I started out by asking him the Morning Power Questions, then the Problem-Solving Questions.

First I asked him, "What are you happy about? I know that sounds stupid and ridiculous and Pollyannaish, but what are you really happy about?" His first response was, "Nothing."

So I said, "What *could* you be happy about right now *if you wanted to be?*" He thought a few moments, then said, "I'm really happy about my wife, because she's doing really well right now, and our relationship is really close." Then I asked him, *"How does that make you feel* when you think of how close you are with her?" He said, "It's one of the most incredible gifts in my life." I said, "She's a special lady, isn't she?" He started focusing on his feelings about her, and he immediately began to feel better.

You might say that I was just distracting him, but I was really helping him to get into a better emotional state, and in a better state you can come up with better ways of dealing with things.

So I asked him what else he was happy about. He started talking about how he *should* be happy that he'd just helped a writer close his first book deal, and how delighted the writer was. He told me that he should feel proud, but he didn't.

"If you did feel proud," I asked him, *"how would that feel?"*

As he thought about how great that would feel, his emotional state began to change. I then asked, "What else are you proud of?" He said, "I'm really proud of my kids. They really care about people, and they take care of themselves. I'm proud of who they've become as men and women and that they're my children. They're part of my legacy."

"How does it make you feel to know that you've had that impact?" I asked, and this man—who'd earlier believed that his life was over—came alive.

Then I asked him what he was grateful for. He said

that he was really grateful that he'd made it through the tough times when he was a young and struggling lawyer, that he'd built his career from the bottom up, and that he'd lived the "American dream." Then I asked, "What are you really excited about?" He said, **"Actually, I'm excited that I have an opportunity right now to make a change."**

That was the first time he'd thought about that, and he had done so because he'd changed his state so radically. I asked him, "Whom do you love, and who loves you?" He started talking about his family and how incredibly close they were.

Then I asked him a really tough question: "What's *great* about your partner leaving?" He said, "You know, what could be great about this is that I hate coming into the city every day, and I love being at my home in Connecticut. **What's also great about this is that I get to look at everything in a new way."** This made him think of a whole string of possibilities, and he decided to set up a new office in Connecticut just five minutes from his home, bring his son into the business, and have an answering service pick up his calls in Manhattan. He got so excited that he decided to look for a new office immediately.

In a matter of minutes, the power of questions had worked their magic. Had his resources always been available to him? Of course, but the questions he'd been asking had made him feel helpless, causing him to see himself as an old man who'd lost everything he'd built. In reality, life had given him a tremendous gift, but he hadn't been able to see the truth until he started asking quality questions.

Another life-changing tool is your physiology. What's that? Let me tell you about it. . . .

Lesson Seven
WELCOME TO THE GREAT STATE OF . . . YOU!

Most of us realize that the way we feel emotionally affects the way we feel physically. But few of us realize how powerfully the reverse is true: when we are moved physically, we are moved emotionally, too. The two cannot be separated.

We all must realize that emotion is created by motion. The way we move changes the way we think, feel, and behave. Movement affects our body's chemistry, including everything from more physical activities (such as running, clapping, or jumping) to the smallest movements in the muscles of the face.

How does a person who is depressed, for example, look to you? If you've ever been depressed, how did your own body look? In order to *feel* depressed, don't you have to use your *body* in a certain way? What must you do with your shoulders, slouch forward or pull them back? The answer is obvious, isn't it? Where is your head . . . down? Where are your eyes . . . down? Is your breathing shallow? In order to be depressed, it takes effort. You know what you're like when you're depressed, because you've practiced it at some point in the past, haven't you? We all have. Even Charlie Brown.

Here's the interesting thing. While many researchers have studied how the body can be affected by emotions, only recently have they become interested in how emotions are affected by the body. One of these studies concluded that it's not as significant to know that we smile when we feel good or laugh when we're in good

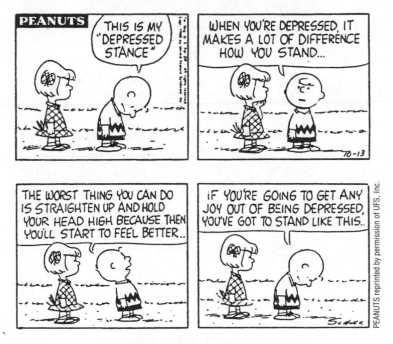

©1960 *United Feature Syndicate, Inc.*

spirits as it is to know that smiling and laughing set off biological processes that, in fact, make us feel good. They increase the flow of blood to the brain and change the level of oxygen, the level of stimulation of the brain's messengers, or *neurotransmitters*. The same thing happens with other expressions. Put your facial expression in the physiology of fear or anger or disgust or surprise, and that's what you'll feel.

Years ago, one of the most important ways I changed my life was to change the pattern of the way I moved, the way I gestured, the way I spoke. At first, I thought this was kind of silly and a little like "putting on airs," but what I found was that by moving my body in new ways, I literally sent a message through my nervous system back to my brain about what I expected from myself. It began to change my feelings and mindset. I began to think more dynamic thoughts and take more powerful, positive, and aggressive actions. But the secret was doing this consciously and deliberately in the beginning and until these unfamiliar movements became my own. Eventually, I didn't have to think about them anymore. I wasn't acting. They were simply powerful, positive habits within my mind and nervous system.

My movements were simply copies of what I had seen other, extremely confident people do. All I did was mimic them with the same kind of intensity and force. This gave me a whole new look at life, and it also made me much more persuasive. I was able to start positively influencing not only myself but also my friends and business associates.

Maybe this sounds overly simplistic to you—change the way you move, and you'll change your life—but it is absolutely accurate. The bigger the change in your movement, the bigger the change in your emotions and actions every day. Here's a suggestion: The next time you start to feel frustrated, jump up for a second, shake your body out, take a deep breath, put a silly grin on your face for no good reason, and ask yourself, "What's great about this?" "What's crazy about this?" "What's funny about this?" "Will this 'problem' even matter ten years from now?" Changing both your physiology and your focus will put you in a much better state of mind. With a new outlook, you can handle whatever's bothering you much more effectively.

Can you think of someone who moves in a way that you'd like to? Are there friends, family members, teachers, actors, dancers, speakers, or other powerful role models that you could imitate? Imagine this person. Even if you're not sure exactly how this person would move or speak, can't you come up with a good idea?

Suppose you're a star quarterback and you've just made the winning touchdown at the Super Bowl. How would you walk? Would your head be down and your shoulders slumped over? No way! You'd be struttin'! Your whole body would say, "I'm the greatest!" Would that change how you feel and what you do? No doubt about it!

You'll find that by moving in the same way that someone else does, you'll start to have very much the same feelings. Right now, before you go on to the next chapter, try this. Stand up, and as you're reading this page, think about a goal or desire you have, something you really want to have happen in your life. As you think about it, start *hoping* for it. Stand the way you stand when you hope, when you're not sure if things will work out. *You hope it works. You hope it doesn't get screwed up.* How do you breathe when you're not sure, when you're just hoping? What does your face look like when you're hoping? Where are your shoulders when you're hoping? Where is the weight in your body? What do you picture when you're just hoping you can achieve a goal? Do you see it working and also not working? Try it now. Don't just read these words on the page.

Now imagine that you're *worried.* Deliberately start worrying about your goal, just for a few moments to see what you have to do with your body. What do you do with your hands to get worried? What happens to your shoulders? Do you have any tension in your body? Do you slow down or restrict your breathing? What happens to the muscles in your face? What does your voice sound like when you're worried? What do you picture? Do you

see it only not working? Do you see the worst-case sce-
nario in your mind? Again, actually put yourself in this
state now, and notice what you do with your body in
order to feel worried.

Now get out of that state and start feeling certain.
Think about your goal and, right now, breathe and stand
the way you would if you were absolutely certain you
could achieve it. How would you stand if there were no
question in your mind whatsoever? What would your
posture be? Put yourself in that place now, even as you
read these words. How would you breathe? What kind of
look would you put on your face? What do you do with
your hands when you're absolutely certain you're going
to achieve what you want?

What is your posture like now? Very different from
hope and worry, isn't it? Where is the weight in your
body? Is it balanced? If you're really certain, you'll probably feel quite grounded and centered. What are you pic-
turing? I bet you don't see it not working but only see it
working.

How can you feel this way every day? Find those
who are successful and model the physiology of their
confidence: their gestures, their breathing, their walk.
Better yet, model the physical movements that you use
yourself when you're in a peak state of mind or emotion.
You'll find that this is not just a game but a way of tapping
into the amazing intelligence that is built into every cell
in your brain and body. You sow the same seeds of movement and breath, and you will reap similar rewards.

And as long as you're meeting role models of confidence, success, and happiness, don't just notice their
physiology but also begin to listen to them. Listen to the
structure of their language, and you'll learn to develop . . .

Lesson Eight
THE VOCABULARY OF SUCCESS

Several years ago, I had an eye-opening business meeting during which I learned the awesome power of words. I was with two men I'd known a long time, and we had just found out that a business associate had tried to take advantage of us. I felt upset about the situation. I suppose you could even say I was angry.

One partner was so mad, he was turning red. "I'm *furious!*" he snapped. I asked him why he felt so angry. "Because if you're really mad, you get really strong and you can turn anything around!"

But my other partner just sat there. He was "a little bit peeved," he said. *Peeved?* "Why do you feel a little peeved, instead of furious?" I asked him.

"Well, if you get angry, you lose control. And the other guy wins," he said.

Peeved. I thought this was the stupidest word I'd ever heard. How could this successful guy go around using a word like that and still keep a straight face?

The answer was that *he didn't*. He almost seemed to enjoy talking about things that would have driven me crazy. His word had a definite effect on him—and on me. Somehow, saying "peeved" made me feel less upset.

So I decided to try it out. I left on a business trip, got to my hotel, and found they didn't have a room for me. "Excuse me," I said, "but the longer I stand here, the more I feel myself getting *peeved.*" The clerk looked up, not quite knowing how to react, and smiled in spite of himself. I had to smile back.

Over the next few weeks, I used this word again and

again. Each time, I thought it was so stupid that it broke my pattern of anger or frustration, and it immediately lowered my emotional intensity.

It was just one word. But how we talk to ourselves —the specific words we use—controls the way we think. And the way we think controls how we feel and what we do.

If you say you're "angry," "pissed off," and "devastated," what kinds of feelings are you going to have? What kinds of questions will you be asking yourself? What will you be focusing on? Won't your blood pressure be going through the roof?

But suppose, instead of "angry," you're "peeved"? Instead of "overwhelmed," you're "in demand"? Instead of "pissed off," you're "tinkled"? Instead of "irritated," you're "stimulated"? Instead of "rejected," you're "misunderstood"? And instead of "devastated," you're "mildly annoyed"? Do you think you'd start feeling different? You'd better believe it!

Maybe this tool sounds inanely simple. It couldn't be that easy to change how we feel just by changing our language! But the truth is that words do have the power to change how we feel. That's why we're so moved when we hear, even decades later, the words of Martin Luther King, Jr. talking about his dream, or John F. Kennedy talking about what one person can do for an entire country. Words change the way we feel, and most of us have no conscious awareness of the ones we're using as we communicate with others—and ourselves—daily, much less how they're affecting the way we think and feel moment to moment. If, for example, you were told that you're *mistaken* about something, you might have one reaction. If you're told you're *wrong*, you might have a more intense reaction. If you're told you're *lying*—

although that's essentially the same statement—just by changing one word, the way you think and feel could be changed in a moment, couldn't it?

Feelin' Groovy

It works the other way, too. You can turn up the volume on happy emotions simply by changing how you describe them.

Feel "ecstatic" instead of just "okay." Be "enthralled" instead of just "interested." Feel "superb" instead of "all right." Instead of feeling "fine," feel "phenomenal"! You're not just "determined," you're "unstoppable"!

So get ready for a new kind of vocabulary test. Come up with some words you use to describe your life that make you feel lousy. Then think of some new words

You can turn up the volume on happy emotions simply by changing how you describe them.

you could use instead. Make them silly, if you want. Have fun!

Old, Disempowering Word	New, Empowering Word
stupid	discovering

I'm sure that you've got some great words! Just to give you a few more ideas, here's a list of some that I've heard through the years:

Negative Emotion/ Expression	Transforms Into
angry	disenchanted
depressed	calm before action
disappointed	delayed
embarrassed	aware
that stinks	that's a little aromatic
failed	learned something
lost	searching
terrible	different

Now come up with some words that really turbo-charge your experience. Turn your okay words into real sparklers!

Old, Boring Word	New, Exciting Word
interesting	amazing

Here are some examples:

Positive Word/ Expression	Transforms into
awake	energized
cool	outrageous
pretty good	unstoppable
fortunate	unbelievably blessed
good	can't get any better
okay	super
quick	explosive
smart	brilliant
tasty	sumptuous

Start using your new choices right away. Make sure you're having a "blast," and you're not just "killing time." If you're having trouble with this, you may need to answer the question . . .

Lesson Nine
ARE YOU
"UP AGAINST A WALL"?
BREAK THROUGH WITH
A NEW METAPHOR!

"I'm at the end of my rope."
"I can't break through the wall."
"My head is about to burst."
"I'm at a crossroads."
"I struck out."
"I'm floating on air."
"I'm drowning."
"I'm happy as a lark."
"I've reached a dead end."
"I'm carrying the world on my shoulders."
"Life is a bowl of cherries."

What do all of these statements have in common? They're *metaphors*. Just what is a metaphor? Whenever you describe something as being like something else, you're creating a metaphor. Metaphors are like symbols: a quick way to say a lot. People use metaphors all the time to describe how they feel about all kinds of things.

"Life is a battle" and "life is a beach" are two metaphors and two very different ways of looking at the world. What goes along with thinking life is a battle? If you described life that way, you'd probably believe that people are always fighting one another.

"Life is a game."

But if you said life was a beach, you might believe people could have fun together!

Metaphors That Make a Difference

Behind every metaphor is a system of beliefs. **When you choose a metaphor to describe your life or your situation, you choose the beliefs it supports, too.** This is why you want to be careful about the way you describe your world—to yourself or to anyone else.

Two people who have metaphors that I admire are the actor Martin Sheen and his wife, Janet. Their metaphor for humanity is that of "one giant family." As a result, they feel the deepest caring and compassion, even for complete strangers.

I remember when Martin shared with me the moving story of how his life changed years ago while he was making the movie *Apocalypse Now*. Before then, he had seen life as something to fear. Now he sees it as an intriguing challenge. Why? His new metaphor is "Life is a mystery."

What changed his metaphor? Intense pain. They had been filming under a grueling schedule deep in the jungles of the Philippines. After a restless night, he woke up the next morning and realized he was suffering a massive heart attack. Portions of his body were numb and paralyzed. He fell to the ground and, through nothing but the sheer power of his will, crawled to the door and managed to get help.

Through the efforts of the film crew, doctors, and even a stunt pilot, Martin was flown to a hospital for emergency care. Janet rushed to his side. He was becoming weaker with each moment. She refused to accept the graveness of his condition—she knew that Martin needed strength—so she smiled brightly at him and said, "It's just a movie, babe! It's only a movie."

Martin has told me that in that moment, he knew he was going to make it. He couldn't laugh, but he began to smile, and with the smile, he began to heal.

What a great metaphor! In movies, people don't *really* die, do they? In a movie, *you* can decide how it all turns out.

I can hear you saying, "This all *sounds* great, but right now, I really feel like I'm fenced in." Great! Just find the gate and open it. "Yeah," you might say, "but I'm carrying the weight of the world on my shoulders." So set the world down and move on!

How do you describe *your* world? Is it a test? Is it a struggle? What if it were a dance? Or a game? Or a flower garden?

If life were a dance, what would that mean? You'd have partners, graceful movement, and harmony. What if life were a game? It would be fun; it would be a chance for you to play with other people; it could even mean there are rules—and winners. What if life were a flower garden? Think of the brilliant colors, the alluring fragrance, the natural beauty! Could you enjoy life a little more in such a garden?

What do you think you'd need to do to make your life *whatever* you want it to be? You must first get . . .

Lesson Ten
READY . . . SET . . . GOAL!
HOW SETTING GOALS
CAN BUILD YOUR FUTURE

When people achieve extraordinary, seemingly impossible goals, they're often assumed to have been "fortunate," "in the right place at the right time," or "born under a lucky star." But I've interviewed many of the greatest achievers in the world, and one of the interesting things I've learned is that each of their incredible accomplishments began with the same first step: the setting of a goal.

For example, when I met Michael Jordan, I asked him what he thought set him apart from other players, what it was that had advanced him time and time again to personal and team victories. What made him the best? Was it God-given talent? Was it skill? Was it strategy? Michael told me, "Many people have God-given talent, and I'm certainly one of them. But what has set me apart throughout my entire life is that you'll never find anyone more competitive than I am. I will not settle for second in anything."

You're probably wondering, as I did, about the source of that fierce competitiveness. One of the turning points occurred when Michael was in tenth grade, after a temporary defeat spurred him to strive for a huge goal. You see, what most people don't know is that Michael— Air Jordan, Mr. All-State, All-American, All-NBA, one of the greatest basketball players of all time, the legend who changed the game forever—didn't even make his high school varsity basketball team.

On the day Michael was cut from the Laney High School Buccaneers, he went home and cried the rest of the afternoon. It would have been easy to give up after that huge disappointment. But instead, he turned this painful experience into a burning desire: he set a higher standard, an even greater goal for himself. He made a real and powerful decision—one that would shape his destiny and the destiny of the sport. He determined he would not only make the team but also be the best player on the court.

To achieve this ambitious goal, he did what every other successful man or woman does: he set a goal then took immediate and massive action. During the summer before his junior year, he sought the help of the team's coach, Clifton Herring, and every morning at 6 A.M., Coach Herring drove Michael to the court and put him through intensive drills. At about the same time, the budding basketball player grew to 6 feet 2 inches. In fact, Michael's desire to achieve his goal was so intense that he would hang on the monkey bars at school trying to elongate his body because he thought it would help him make the team. (This just shows you the power of "stretching" yourself!)

Michael practiced every day, and when the time came, he was chosen to play for the varsity team. He proved a point that his Chicago Bulls coach Doug Collins would make about him more than a decade later: **The harder you prepare, the luckier you seem to get.** Some people are afraid to set goals because they think that they'll be disappointed or fail. What they don't realize is that achieving the goal isn't half as important as setting it, then taking massive action toward its attainment. **The**

reason we set goals is to give our lives focus and to move us in the direction we would like to go. Ultimately, whether or not you achieve a goal is not half as important as the type of person you become in pursuit of it.

Choosing a goal may cause only a slight change in your life's direction at first. It's like one of those huge freighters at sea: If the captain shifts course by just a few degrees, it won't be noticeable immediately. But in several hours or days, this change in direction will bring the ship to a completely different destination.

In order to get out of the dumps more than a decade ago, I had to make a lot of changes in direction and set a lot of goals, too. As I worked toward all of them (getting in shape, building confidence, etc.), I learned something superimportant; my success depended on doing my best —not just once in a while but *consistently.*

All people who succeed dedicate themselves to *continuous* improvement. They're never satisfied with just doing well; they constantly want to do better. If you dedicate yourself to this philosophy of constant and never-ending improvement, or what I call CANI!™ (pronounced kuhn-EYE), then you can virtually guarantee that you'll not only continue your growth throughout your life—the real source of happiness—but you'll also succeed. By the way, CANI! does not mean that you do everything perfectly, nor does it mean that everything changes instantly. The most successful people are those who understand the power of "chunking," who don't bite off more than they can chew at one time. In other words, they break a goal down into bite-size pieces, achievable "subgoals" that lead toward the ultimate success they desire. But it's not enough just to set subgoals; you have to celebrate the achievement of each small step. This will

*In order to get out of the dumps, you have to set
a lot of goals.*

help you build momentum and develop habits that will
gradually turn your dreams into reality.

　　We've all heard that a journey of a thousand miles
starts with a single step. But we often forget to remind

ourselves of that while we're setting a goal. When was the last time you gave yourself a pat on the back just for taking a small step in the direction you wanted to go? Years ago, I didn't wait until I'd lost all 38 pounds before rewarding myself. At first, just pushing the plate away with food on it was a big deal—a real accomplishment! So, for example, if you just talk to five people today about a career move you're thinking about making, and you gather information that can help you make a decision, then that's five steps forward. Even if you don't make that career move today, you are still moving in a new direction. Remember that what you did in the past does not determine what you'll do in the future.

As a very famous poem says, *you* are the master of your fate; *you* are the captain of your soul. It's up to you. Don't wait to set your goals. Start turning your freighter *now*, because up ahead, just a short distance away, is your future.

A Future Worth Fighting For

What makes some people willing to take action, even when they're feeling down or afraid? Why do certain individuals overcome tremendous obstacles? How do they bounce back from what others call defeat, again and again?

They have a future worth fighting for—a *compelling future.*

Take my friend W. Mitchell, for example. In a terrible motorcycle accident, two-thirds of his body was burned. As he lay in the hospital, he decided he'd figure out a way to contribute to the people around him, no matter what. Even though his face had been burned beyond recognition, he believed his smile could light up their world. And it did. He believed he could cheer people up; he could listen to people and comfort them. And he did.

A few years later he was in another accident, this time in a plane, that paralyzed him from the waist down. Did he give up? No. Instead, he noticed a beautiful nurse at the hospital. "How could I get a date with her?" he asked. His buddies told him he was nuts. Maybe he secretly agreed with them. But he didn't stop dreaming.

W. Mitchell saw a great future with this beautiful woman. He used his charm, his fine wit, his free spirit, and his dynamic personality to attract her, and he eventually ended up marrying her. Most people in his position would never have even tried. But he reached for the stars —and changed his life forever.

How did he create his compelling future? He set goals that went far beyond what he thought he could really accomplish. He made a decision that, no matter what, he would achieve those goals. He made it believable by breaking that goal down into small, bite-size chunks: tiny, minute movements that he needed to accomplish daily before he could make the more dynamic movements forward in his life. When you choose a truly inspiring goal, you free the power within yourself to achieve far more than others imagine is possible. You give yourself an incredible opportunity to stretch and grow.

"Winning starts with beginning."

—Anonymous

There are people—we all know some of them— who seem constantly lost in a fog of confusion. They go one way, then another. They try one thing, then shift to something else. They move down one path, then retreat in the opposite direction. Their problem is simple: they don't know what they want. You can't hit a target if you don't know what it is.

What you need to do now is dream. But it's absolutely essential that you do so in a totally focused way. If you just read this book, it's not going to do you any good. You need to sit down and put your dreams on paper.

Settle into a comfortable place, somewhere you feel secure and completely at ease. Plan to spend at least half an hour or so discovering what you expect to be and do and share and see and create. It could be the most valuable thirty minutes you ever spend! You're going to learn to set goals and determine outcomes. You're going to make a map of the roads you want to travel in your life. You're going to figure out where you want to go and how you expect to get there.

Let me start with one major warning: There is no need to put any limitations on what's possible.

What would you do if you knew you could not fail? Take a moment to really consider this question. **If you were absolutely certain of success, what activities would you pursue, what actions would you take?**

Be specific. The more detailed you are, the more empowered you are to create a result. As you create your list, some of the things you write down will be things you've thought about for years. Some will be things you've never even dreamed of before. But you need to decide what you really want, because knowing what you want determines what you will get. **Before something happens in the world, it must first happen in your mind.**

No Limits!

In the back of this book you'll find some blank pages. You might find them ideal for this goal-setting session. Let's get down to business:

1. Pretend it's the holiday season—time for giving and receiving abundant gifts! Dream big! Write down *all* your dreams, all of the things you want to have, do, be, and share. Imagine the people, feelings, and places you want to be a part of your life. Sit down right now, grab your pencil, and start writing. Don't try to figure out how you're going to get there; *just write it down.* **There are no limits.**

2. Now go over the list you made and estimate when you expect to reach those outcomes: six months, one year, two years, five years, ten years, twenty years. It's helpful to see what sort of a time frame you're operating in.

Note how your list came out. Some people find that the list they made is dominated by things they want today. Others find their greatest dreams are far in the future, in some perfect world of total success and fulfillment. But a journey of a thousand miles begins with a single step, and it's important to be aware of the first steps as much as the final ones.

3. Once you've set some time frames, pick four goals that you can realize *this year*. Pick the things you're most committed to, most excited about, things that would give you the most satisfaction. On another sheet of paper, write them down again, and also write down *why* **you absolutely will achieve them.** *Why* to do something is much more powerful than *how*—if you get a big enough why, you can always figure out the how.

Think not only about yourself but about others in

your life as well. How would your family or friends bene-
fit if you achieved your goals? If you have enough rea-
sons, you can do virtually anything in this world.

**4. After you've done all this, describe the kind
of person you would have to be to attain your goals.**
Will it take more compassion or more drive? Would you
need to go back to school? If, for example, you wanted
to be a teacher, describe what kind of person really has
the ability to touch others' lives.

Train Your Brain

One of my rules is that **whenever I set a goal, I
take immediate action to support it.** W. Mitchell
started smiling at people the day he decided he'd give
something to the world. He asked that nurse to go out
with him right away.

But romance didn't bloom overnight. Progress will
be step by step for you, too. As your best friend, you
would never beat yourself up because you didn't achieve
your goal right away, would you?

Finally, "train your brain" so it knows this goal is a
happening thing:

- Twice a day, sit quietly for a few minutes and think
  about your goal.
- Imagine that you have already achieved your goal.
  Feel the pleasure, pride, and excitement of this
  fulfillment. See and hear all the wonderful details!

Feels fantastic, doesn't it?

Do you believe in this stuff? Yes? No? Kind of? I'd
like to prove to you that these tools really do work. So
I've made up a kind of game. If you agree to play it full-

out—if you agree to meet all its challenges with all the determination you have—the rewards will be beyond anything you imagined.

Are you ready? Then let's meet . . .

Lesson Eleven
THE TEN-DAY
MENTAL CHALLENGE

If you don't do anything else in this book, **DO THIS!**
I call it the Ten-Day Mental Challenge. This exercise
turned my life right-side up. How?

**It enabled me to take control of my mind by
not allowing myself to hold one negative thought
consistently.**

Are you ready? Here are the rules of the game:

1. During the next ten days, *refuse* to hang on to
any crummy thoughts, feelings, questions, words, or
metaphors.

2. When you catch yourself focusing on the negative—and you will—immediately ask yourself questions to get you to a better place. Start with the
Problem-Solving Questions (on page 57).

3. When you wake up in the morning, ask yourself
the Morning Power Questions (on page 58). Just
before you fall asleep at night, ask yourself the
Evening Power Questions (on page 59). This will do
wonders to keep you feeling good.

4. For the next ten consecutive days, focus *completely* on solutions and not on problems.

5. If you have a lousy thought, question, or feeling,
don't beat yourself up. Just change it immediately.
If you dwell on any of these for more than five minutes, however, *you must wait until the following
morning and start the ten days over.*

*Starting right now, decide to use all the tools in this
book so that you will not dwell on any rotten thoughts
or emotions for the next ten days.*

The goal here is ten *consecutive* days without dwelling on a negative thought. Anytime you dwell too long on the negative, you must start over, no matter how many days in a row you've already met the challenge.

I want you to know that the power of this Ten-Day Mental Challenge is truly amazing. If you stick with it, it will start a parade of benefits in your life that won't stop. Here are just four things it will give you:

1. It will make you see all the mental habits that hold you back.

2. It will make your brain search for powerful, help-ful alternatives.

3. It will give you a tremendous jolt of confidence as you see you can turn your life around.

4. It will create new habits, new standards, and new expectations that will help you grow and enjoy life more and more, every day!

WELCOME TO A CARING WORLD

The first time I took the Ten-Day Mental Challenge, I lasted only about two days! But I can tell you that by holding myself to a higher standard, and by persisting until I succeeded, the Ten-Day Mental Challenge became a life-changing experience. I know that with diligence, it can produce the same level of freedom for you as it has for me.

And now I'd like to offer you a different sort of challenge . . . a special invitation, if you will.

We began this book with the idea that one of the best ways to solve our own problems—to create our own happiness—is to help someone else who's in a tougher position than we are. When people tell me how difficult life is, how their problems seem unsolvable, the first thing I do is help interrupt this habitual mindset. I make a simple request. "I want you to *forget* about your problems for a day or two, look for someone else who is having a rougher time than you are right now, and assist that person in making it 'just a little' better." My advice is often met with a look that says, "There is no one with bigger problems than I have!" But of course, this is never true. If you've lost your job, then go find a couple who has lost their son or daughter. If you're struggling to make ends meet, find someone who is struggling to stay alive on the streets. If you're fretting about a missed promotion, find someone huddling in doorways to seek shelter from the harsh weather, getting sustenance only from soup kitchens. Remember how lucky you really are.

Chances are there is more than one person out there with a more difficult challenge than the one you're currently facing. Helping out will do two things. (1) It will put your problem in perspective. Your burden will probably seem light in comparison, and you'll see firsthand the amazing courage people invariably show in meeting life's greatest challenges. You'll realize that there's always a way to turn things around. (2) Even if you don't "solve" the problem, even if all you do is comfort and care about someone else, you'll learn that you cannot give a gift without receiving one back tenfold. I'm not talking about getting rewarded for your efforts; I'm talking about tapping into one of the deepest human needs: the need for a sense of contribution. Simply by giving unselfishly, you will experience the ultimate in human joy and fulfillment.

So how do you take part in this? Is it difficult? No way! Within the next twenty-four hours—or at the most within the next week—give someone you don't even know a "little bit" of help, a "little bit" of support. Maybe tomorrow you could look in the yellow pages to find a retirement or convalescent home. On your way home from work, instead of getting stuck in traffic, you could stop in, introduce yourself to the person in charge, and ask to see someone who hasn't had a visitor in a while. You could say you'd like to meet someone who doesn't have a family, or someone who does yet never sees them. When you introduce yourself for the first time, give 'em a big smile and say, "Hi, Charlie!" If Charlie's as happy to see you as you are to see him, how about a great big bear hug? Just spend an hour with him, simply talking and listening, finding out who he is and what he's all about. What do you think this would do for a lonely soul, to have a total stranger care enough to come by just to see him? Better yet, what do you think it would do for you?

At a minimum it'll remind you what your life is really about and who you really are. It'll fulfill the most noble and fundamental needs of human nature, to connect and contribute. It'll transform you. So take the time . . . and give yourself the gift that comes only to those who give unselfishly.

As our time together is coming to an end, I'd like to ask you for a personal favor. Promise me that you'll take great care of yourself. The better off you are, the more you'll be able to give to others. Better yet, go beyond just taking care of yourself. Create an extraordinary life—an ordinary life to which you've added just that extra little bit of dedication, commitment, and love.

And please write to tell me how you've used what you've learned here to improve your own or others' lives. I look forward to connecting with you personally. 'Til then . . .

"May the road rise to meet you. May the wind be always at your back. May the sun shine warm on your face, may the rains fall soft upon your fields, and, until we meet again . . . may God hold you softly in the palm of His hand."

—Old Irish Blessing

Goodbye and God Bless,

Anthony Robbins

EPILOGUE

You'll find more information about these ideas in Anthony Robbins' best-selling book, *Awaken the Giant Within.*

Please refer to the following chapters:

"Decisions: The Pathway to Power"
"Belief Systems: The Power to Create and the Power to Destroy"
"How to Get What You Really Want"
"Questions Are the Answer"
"The Vocabulary of Ultimate Success"
"Destroy the Blocks, Break Down the Wall, Let Go of the Rope, and Dance Your Way to Success: The Power of Life Metaphors"
"The Magnificent Obsession—Creating a Compelling Future"
"The Ten-Day Mental Challenge"

For information about how to change your diet and have more energy, please see Chapter 10, "Energy: The Fuel of Excellence," in Anthony Robbins' first book, *Unlimited Power.*

ABOUT THE AUTHOR

Anthony Robbins has devoted more than half his life to helping people discover and develop their own unique qualities of greatness. Considered the nation's leader in the science of peak performance, he is the founder and chairman of the Anthony Robbins Companies, which are committed to assisting people in achieving personal and professional mastery.

Robbins has served as a peak performance consultant for the executives of such organizations as IBM, AT&T, American Express, McDonnell-Douglas, and the United States Army, as well as professional sports teams such as the Los Angeles Dodgers, the Los Angeles Kings, the America³ America's Cup team, and gold medal–winning Olympic athletes. Robbins also provides ongoing coaching and consulting to a number of prominent world figures and is the primary adviser in the regeneration of Sheffield, England's fourth-largest city.

Robbins' special passion is to make the world a better place to live by assisting individuals in captaining their destinies—whether that means fostering their relationships with their families, directing their focus to achieve their goals, relieving emotional or financial distress, or making profound contributions to their communities and country. Throughout the years he has unselfishly given his energy and resources to those in need, and in 1991 he formed a nonprofit foundation to aid underprivileged children, homeless individuals, senior citizens, and the prison population.

Mr. Robbins is thirty-five years old and lives in Del Mar, California, with his wife and children.

ABOUT THE
ANTHONY ROBBINS FOUNDATION

The Anthony Robbins Foundation is a nonprofit organization with a mission to consistently reach and assist homeless individuals, underprivileged children, senior citizens, and the prison population. The finest resources for inspiration, education, training, and development are provided to these important members of our society by all who participate in foundation activities.

A Vision Realized

The foundation is a lifelong dream come true for Anthony Robbins. A committed philanthropist since the age of eighteen, he has worked extensively with the Salvation Army in New York's South Bronx and Brooklyn, as well as with homeless individuals in Hawaii and the San Diego area. (Robbins also continues his personal commitment to fund the entire annual food budget of a social-services agency in San Diego's North County.)

"Champions of Excellence" Scholarship Program

Among the foundation's most inspiring endeavors is the "Champions of Excellence" Scholarship Program. While visiting an elementary school in Houston, Texas, in 1991, Robbins was so touched by the school's students, faculty, and staff that he made a unique pledge: He would pay the college tuition of all fifth-graders (high school graduating class of 1999) who consistently maintained a B average, contributed an average of 43 service hours every year until they graduated college, and met other standards of academic and personal excellence. In response, the children Robbins set out to help have become helpers themselves, tutoring other students, volunteering in nursing homes, staffing shelters, and participating in many other philanthropic endeavors.

Thanksgiving "Basket Brigade"

As a tribute to the American spirit of generosity that benefited his family on Thanksgiving when Robbins was eleven, he has consistently observed the holiday by getting together with family and friends to distribute food and other provisions to those in need. Since the inception of the Anthony Robbins Foundation in 1991, one of its most far-reaching accomplishments has been turning Robbins' personal tradition into a cross-continental effort called the Thanksgiving Basket Brigade. Orchestrated by a network of volunteers, it annually distributes food, clothing, and other resources, and in 1993 alone it reached out to over 100,000 families in more than 400 communities across the United States and Canada.

The Challenge

Life is a gift, and all of us who have the ability must remember that we have the responsibility to give something back. Your contributions can truly make a difference. Please join us now and commit to helping those less fortunate enjoy a greater quality of life.

The foundation's charter is fulfilled through these programs and others like them. People interested in more information about the foundation may write to the Anthony Robbins Foundation at the address on the opposite page, or call 800-445-8183.

9191 Towne Centre Dr.
Suite 600
San Diego, CA 92122

The Anthony Robbins Foundation is a nonprofit organization with tax-exempt status. Contributions to the foundation are tax-deductible.

ABOUT THE
ANTHONY ROBBINS COMPANIES

As an alliance of several organizations sharing the same mission, the Anthony Robbins Companies (ARC) are dedicated to constantly improving the quality of life for individuals and organizations who truly desire it. Offering cutting-edge technologies for the management of human emotion and behavior, ARC empowers individuals to recognize and *utilize* their unlimited choices.

Listed below are just some of the useful resources ARC offers you and/or your organization. For more information and a complete list of available services and products, please call 800-445-8183.

Robbins Research International, Inc.

This research and marketing arm of Anthony Robbins' consulting and personal-development businesses conducts public and corporate seminars all over the world. Topics range from peak performance and financial mastery to negotiating and corporate reengineering.

One of the most sought-after educational experiences promoted by RRI is Robbins' year-round Mastery University. Imparting twenty-first-century leadership skills, this three-part course of instruction is held in some of the most exquisite locales in the world and is taught by a faculty with unmatched qualifications. Some of the instructors and subjects for this program have included General Norman Schwarzkopf on leadership, Dr. Deepak Chopra on health and the mind, and Peter Lynch and Sir John Templeton on finance. The university has been attended by individuals representing forty-two nations.

Anthony Robbins & Associates

This franchise and distributor network brings multimedia seminars to local communities and businesses worldwide.

Owning an Anthony Robbins & Associates franchise offers the opportunity to be a source of positive impact and growth for the members of one's community. Anthony Robbins & Associates provides its franchisees the training, visibility, and ongoing support to create a business that truly makes a difference in people's lives.

Robbins Success Systems™

Robbins Success Systems (RSS) provides *Fortune* 1000 corporations with state-of-the-art management systems, communication, and teamwork training. The RSS team combines thorough pretraining diagnostics, customized facilitation and training, and post-program evaluation and follow-up. Tailored to meet your individual needs, RSS is a catalyst for constant and never-ending improvement in the quality of life within corporations worldwide.

Fortune Practice Management

This full-service professional practice-management company provides health-care professionals with vital strategies and support for increasing the quality and profitability of their practices. Fortune Practice Management is committed to making a difference in the quality of health care and in the quality of life of its practitioners.

Tony Robbins Productions

The focus of this television production company is the creation of the highest-quality direct-marketing infomercials to be broadcast nationally. TRP has worked in joint venture to produce four of the most successful infomercials ever aired. Using sophisticated market analysis, TRP specializes in tailoring products and promotions to meet the unique needs of specific audiences.

Namale Plantation Resort

For many years, the Robbins family has escaped to Fiji, an incredibly beautiful land where the people's highest value is happiness. Now you too can stay at the Robbinses' private paradise—121 acres of tropical island with pristine beaches, magnificent coral reefs, blowholes, and waterfalls. You can snorkel, scuba-dive, water-ski, lie on the beach, ride horses, or play tennis, basketball, and volleyball. Or try bathing under a cool waterfall. Share the music, joy, and warmth of the wonderfully loving Fijian people.

Only twenty people at a time can enjoy this magnificent and private tropical hideaway. After staying at Namale, you'll never look at the world—or yourself— the same way again. If you'd like to visit Namale Plantation Resort, please telephone 011-679-850-435 or your local travel agent for information or reservations.

For a complete list of services available from the Anthony Robbins Companies, please call 800-445-8183.

NOTES

NOTES

NOTES